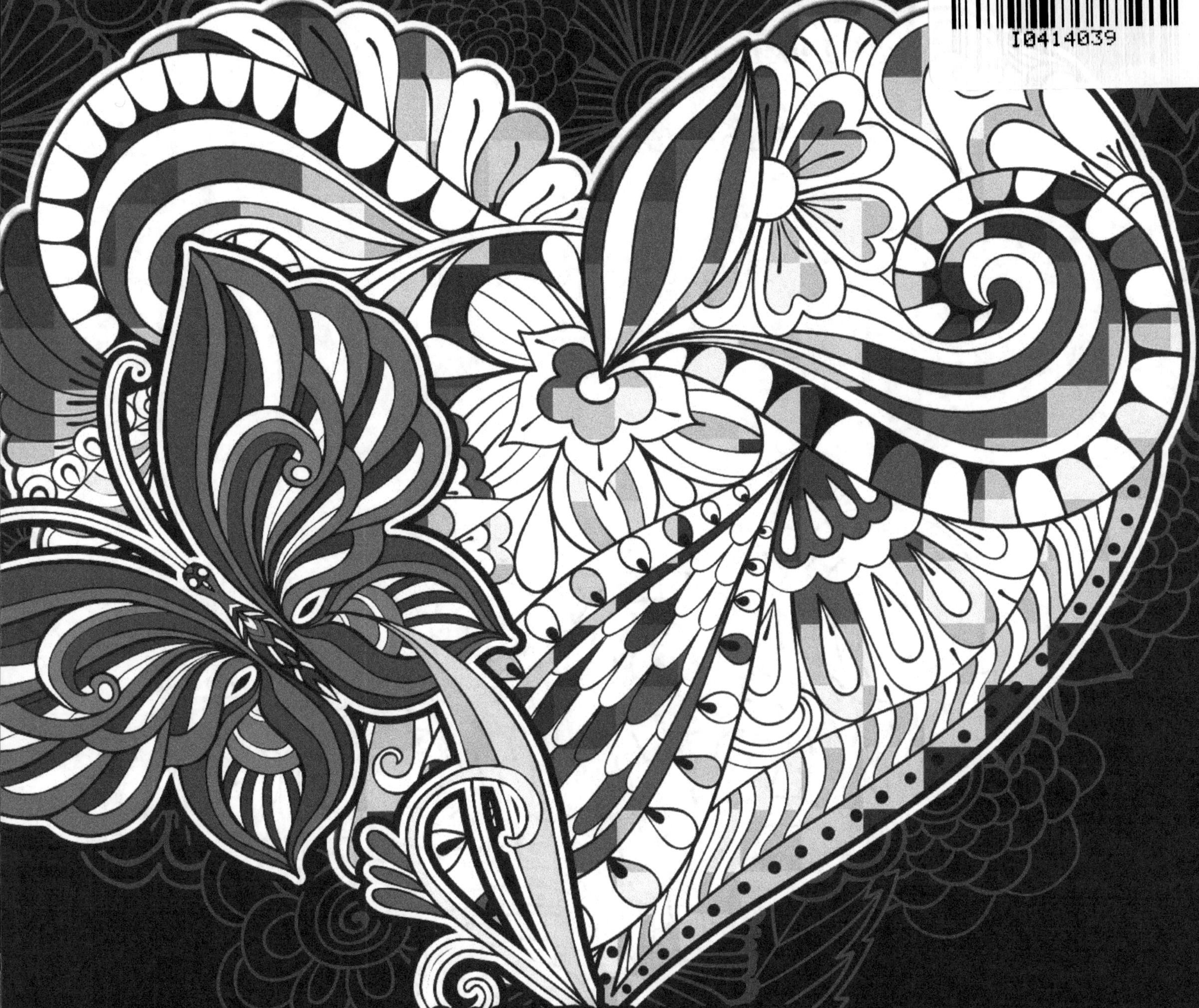

MINDFULNESS

HEART

COLORING BOOK FOR ADULTS

STRESS RELIEVING PATTERNS

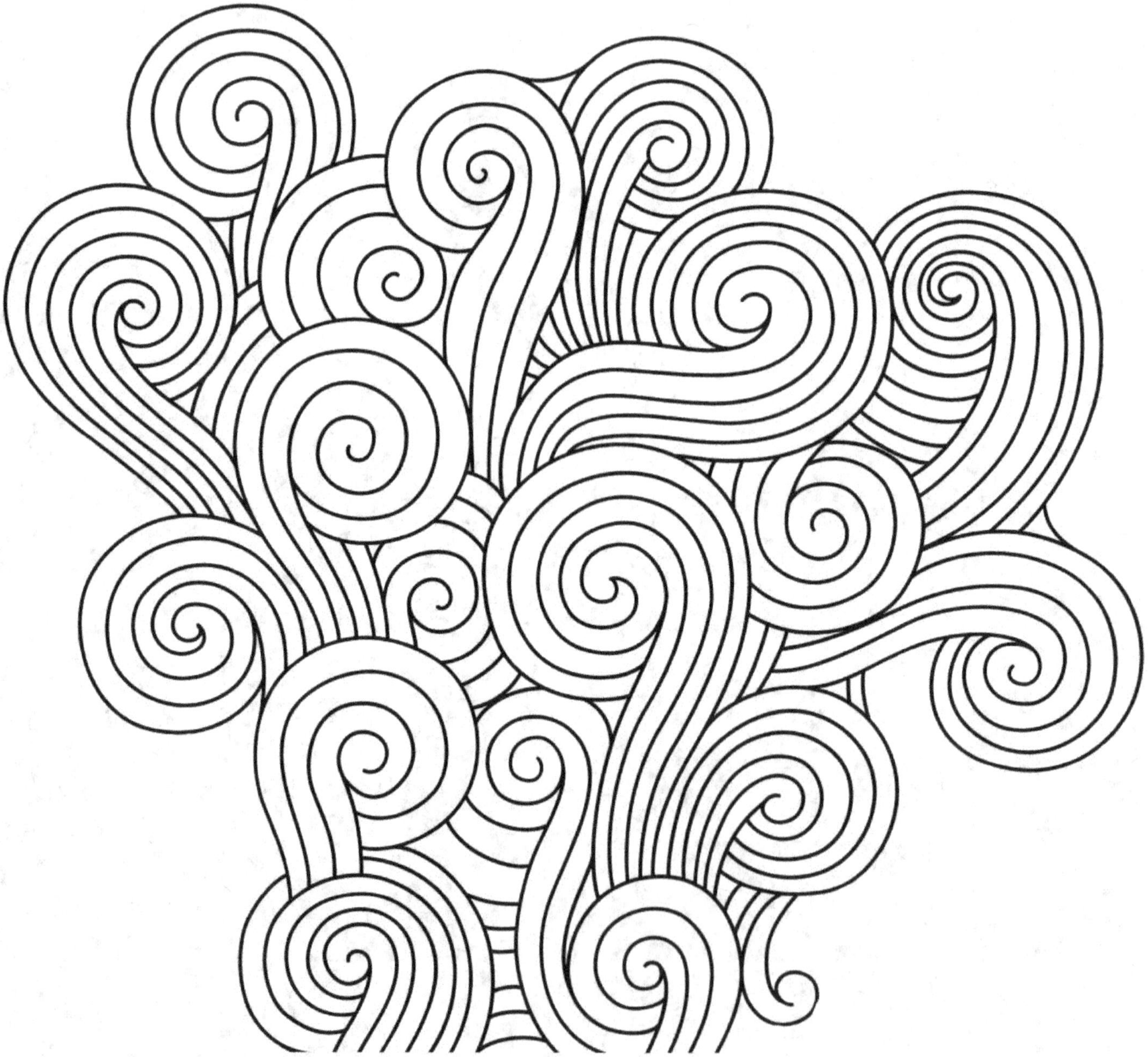

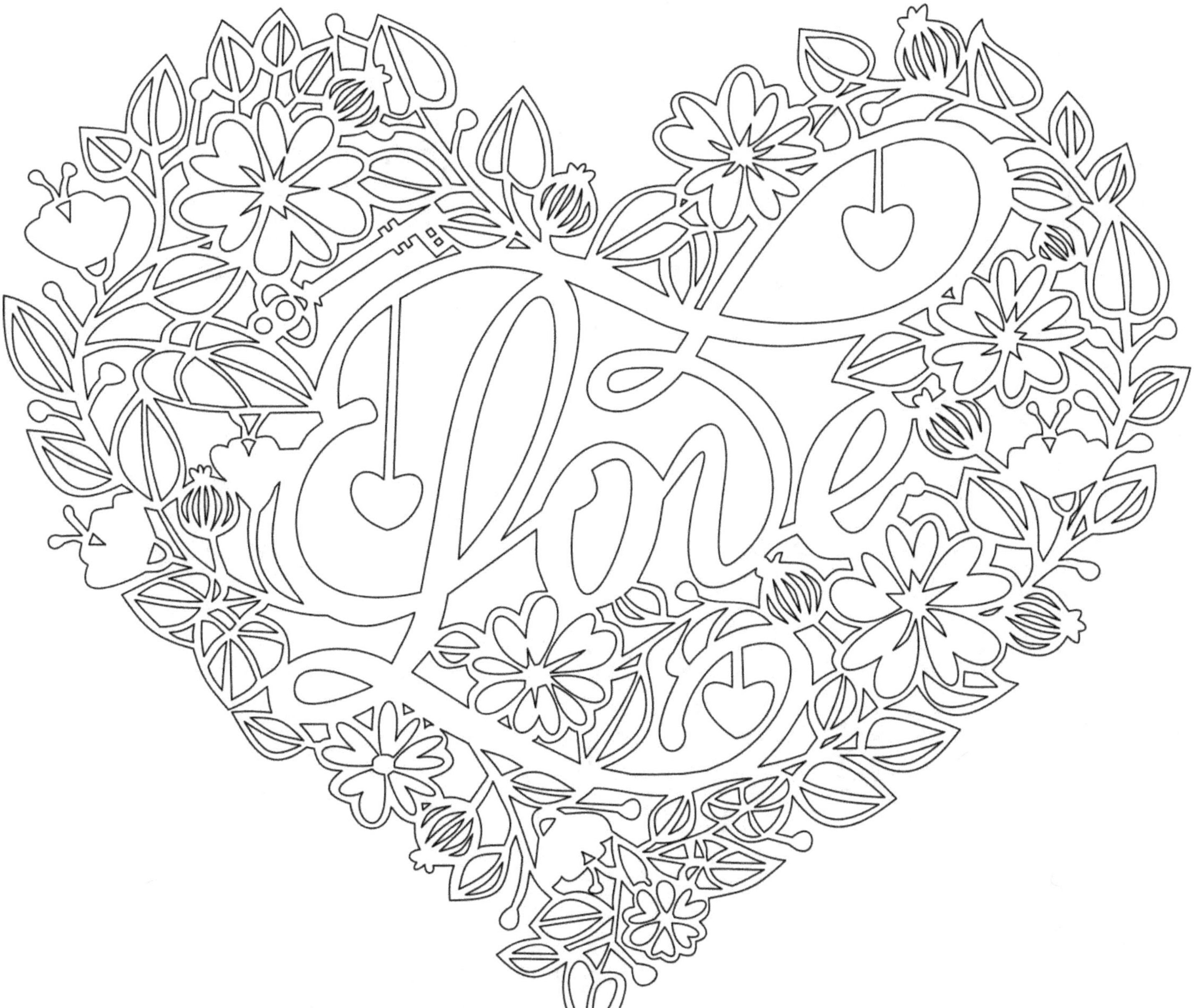
Love

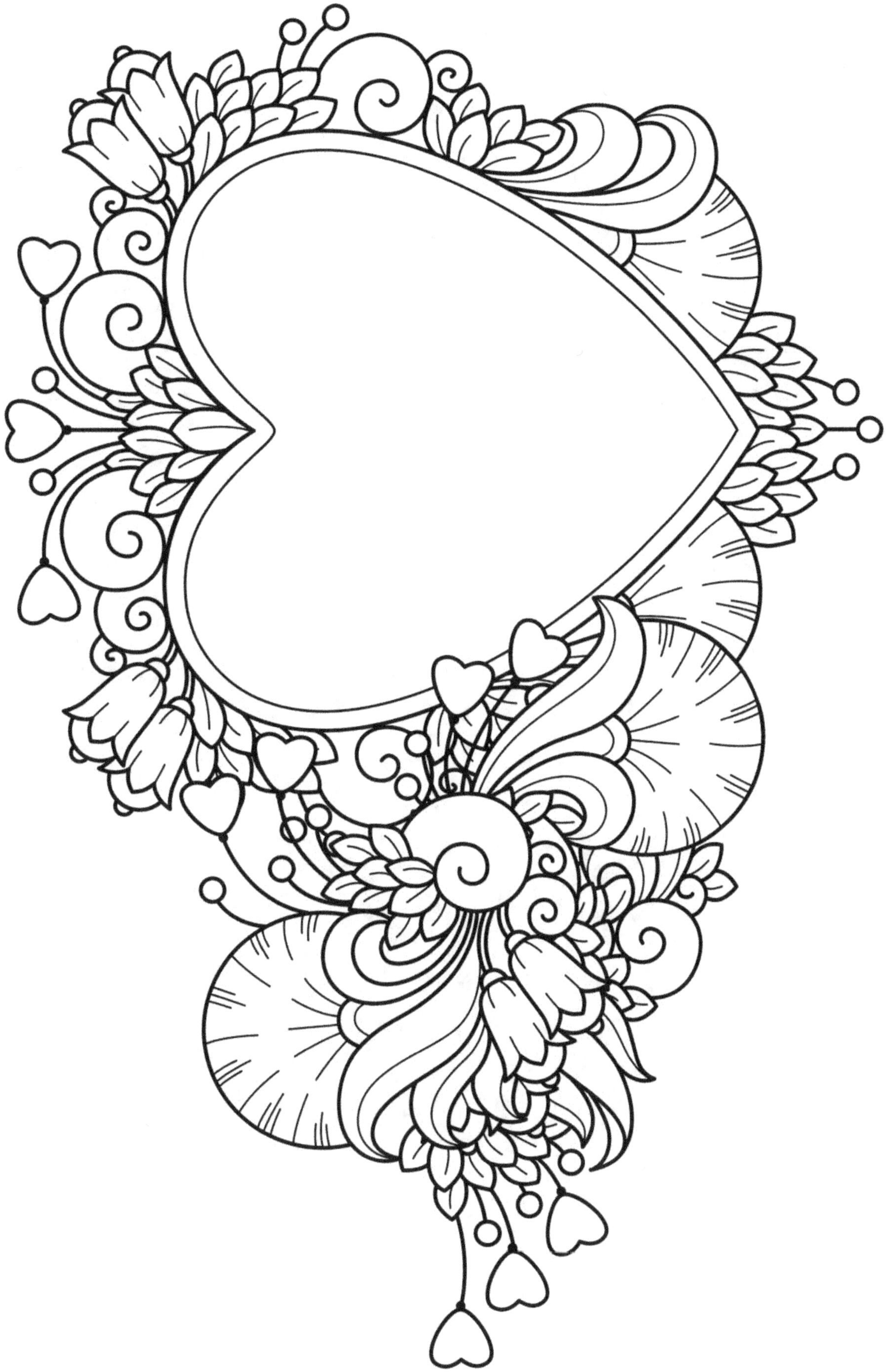

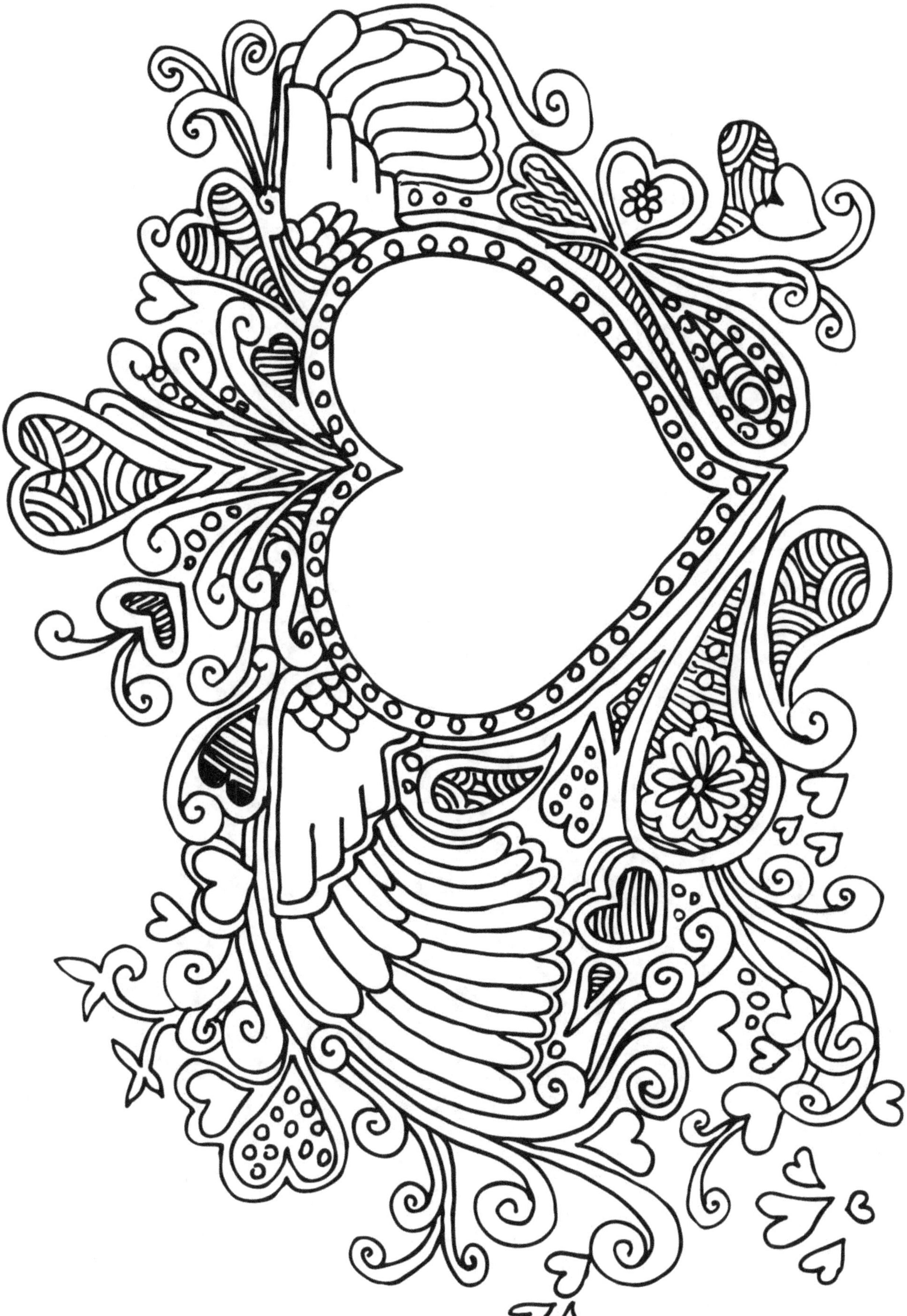

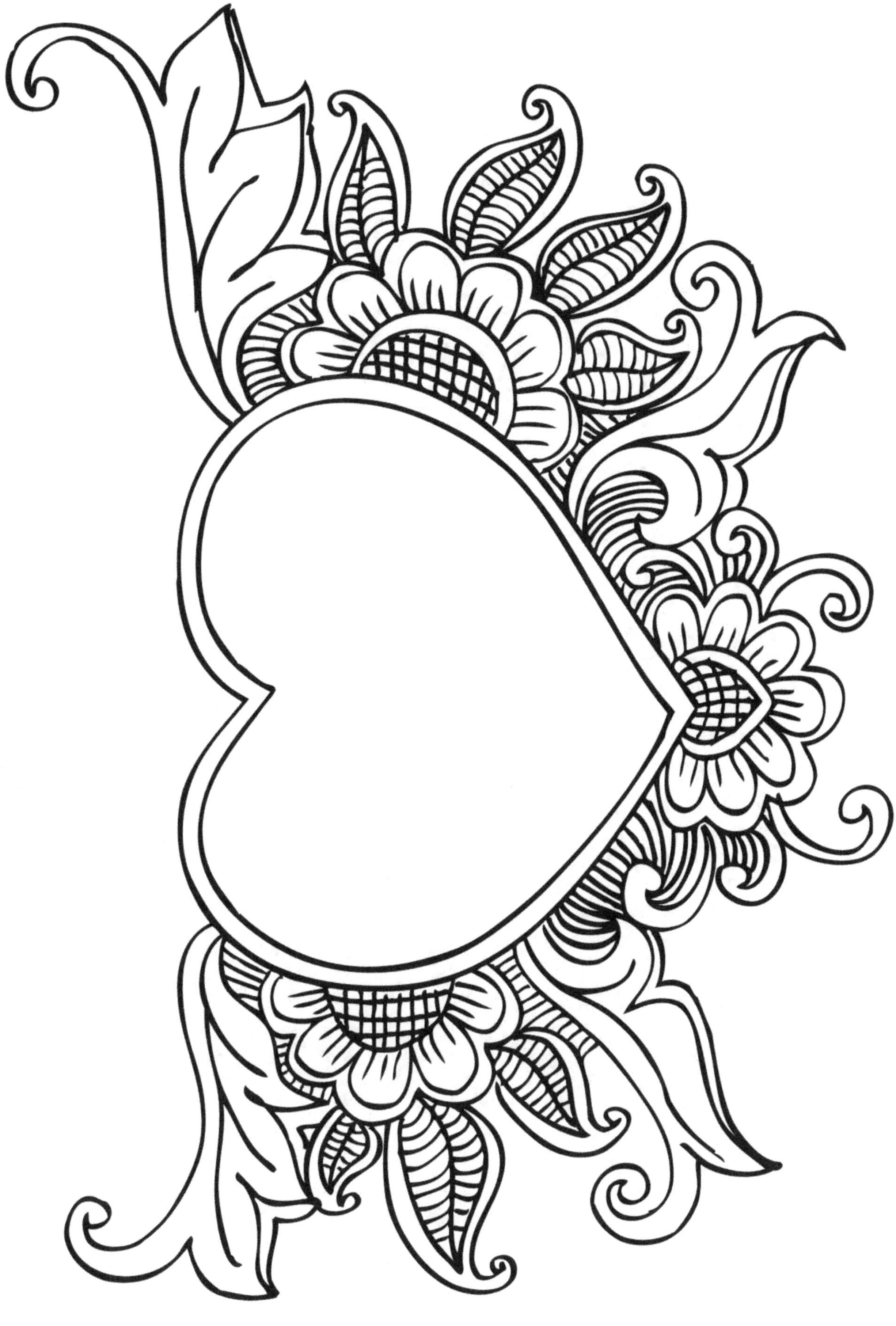

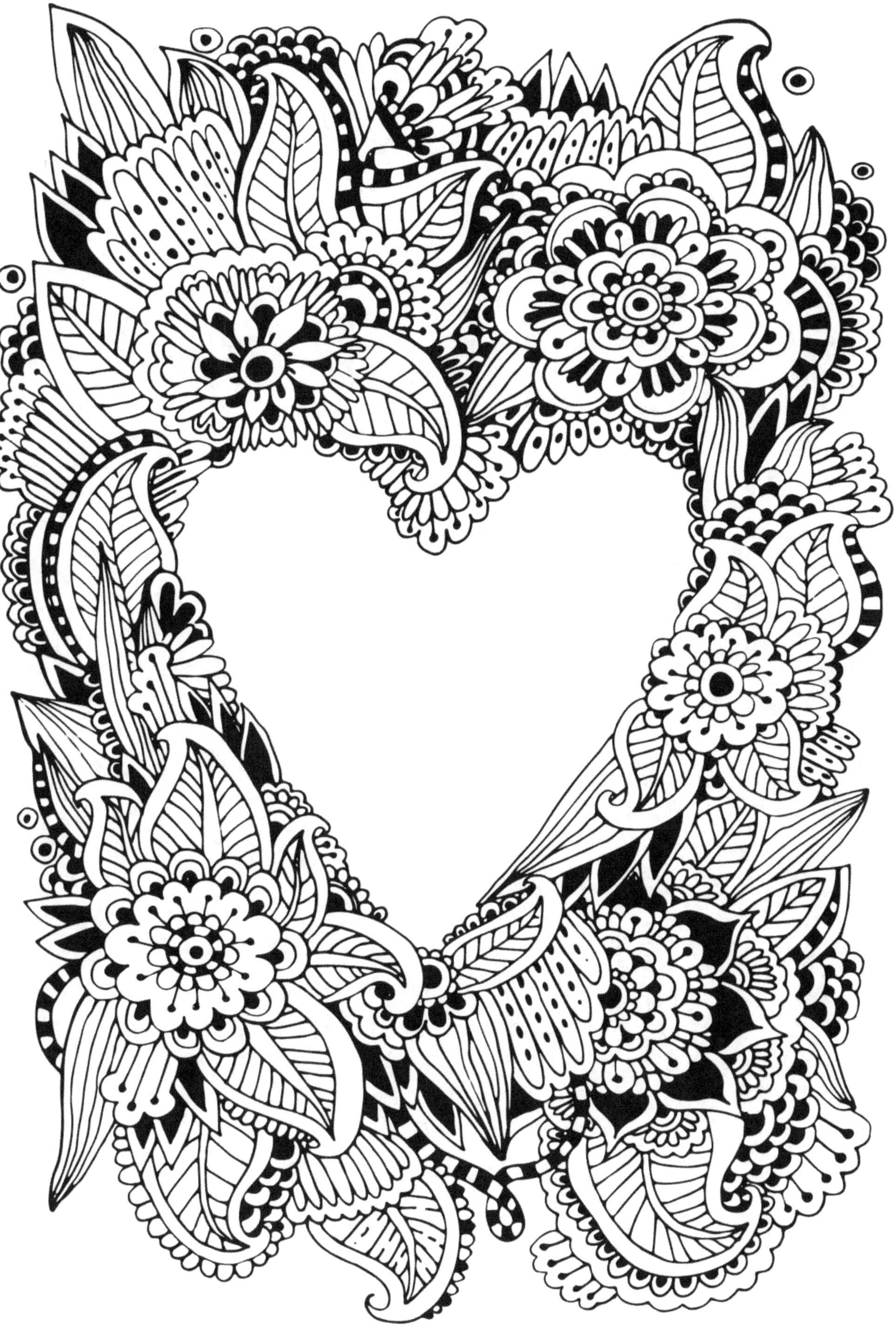

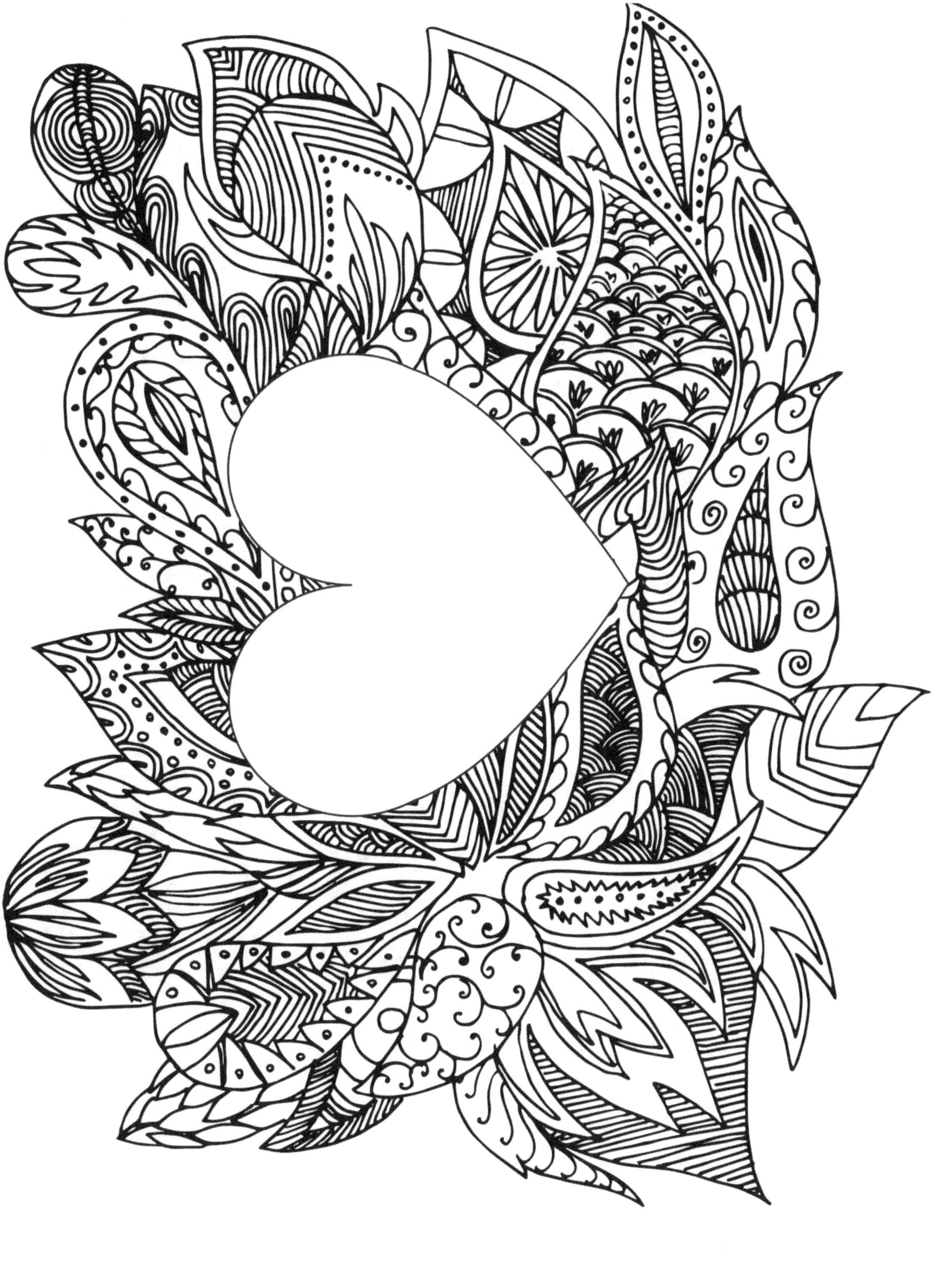

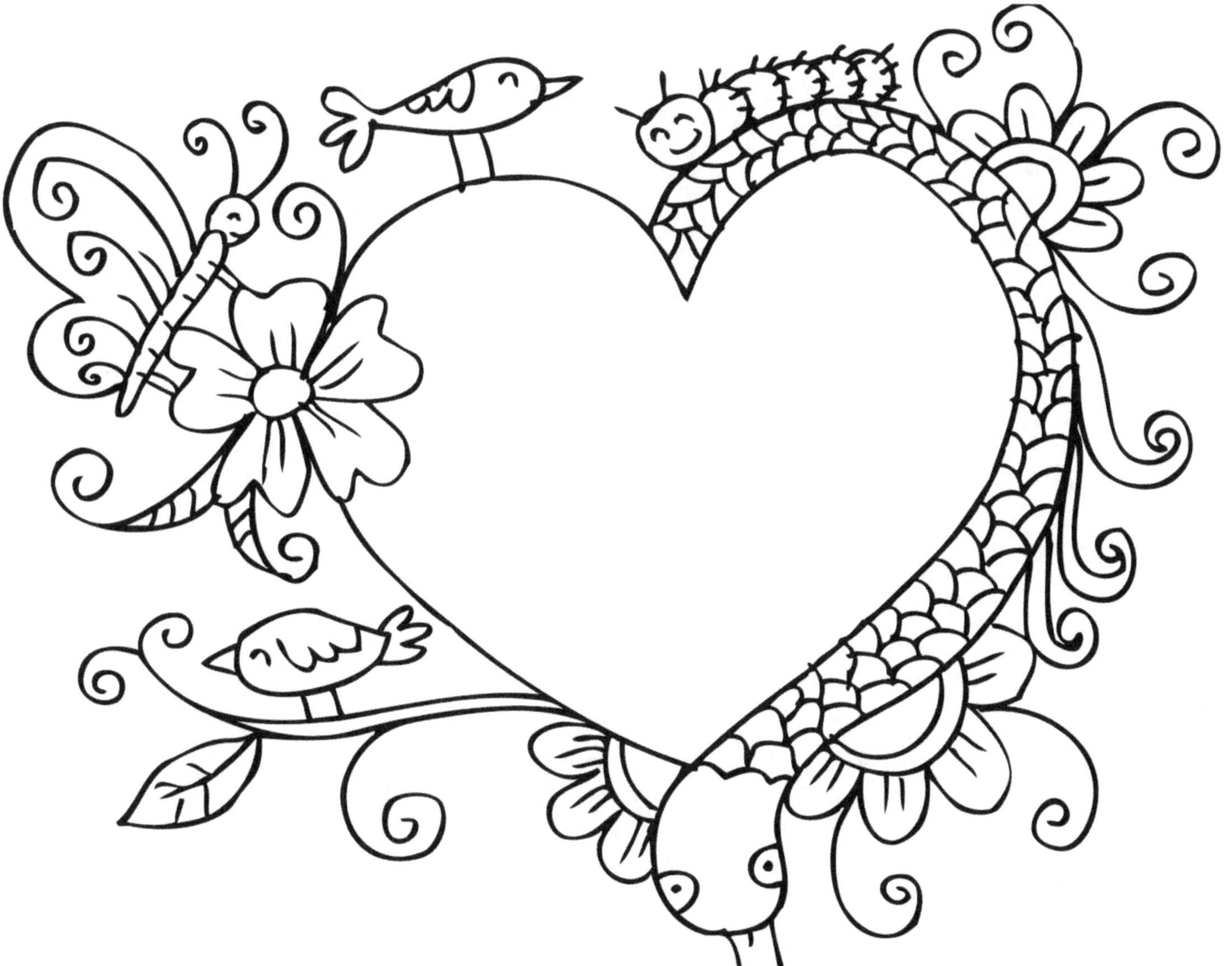

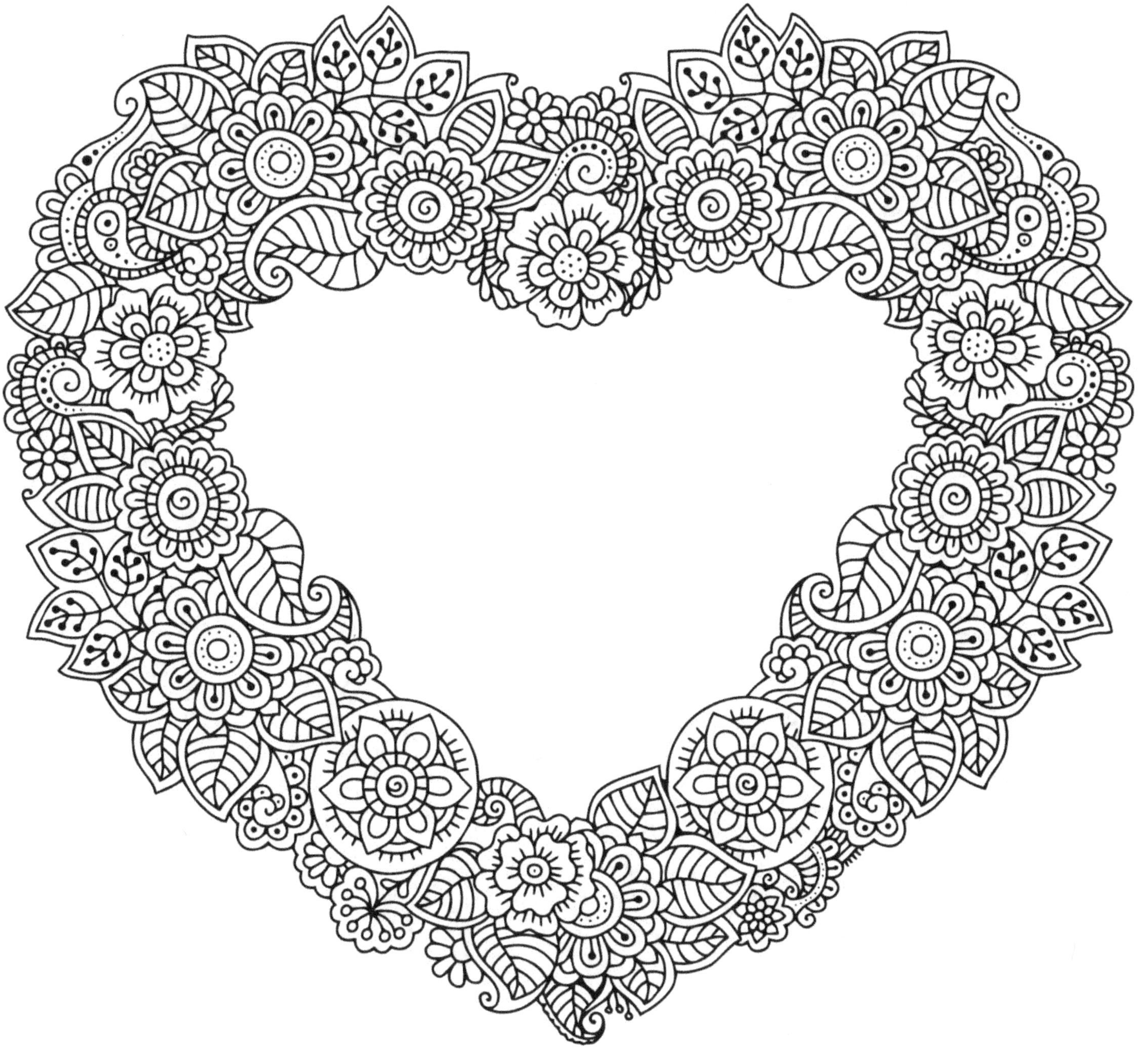

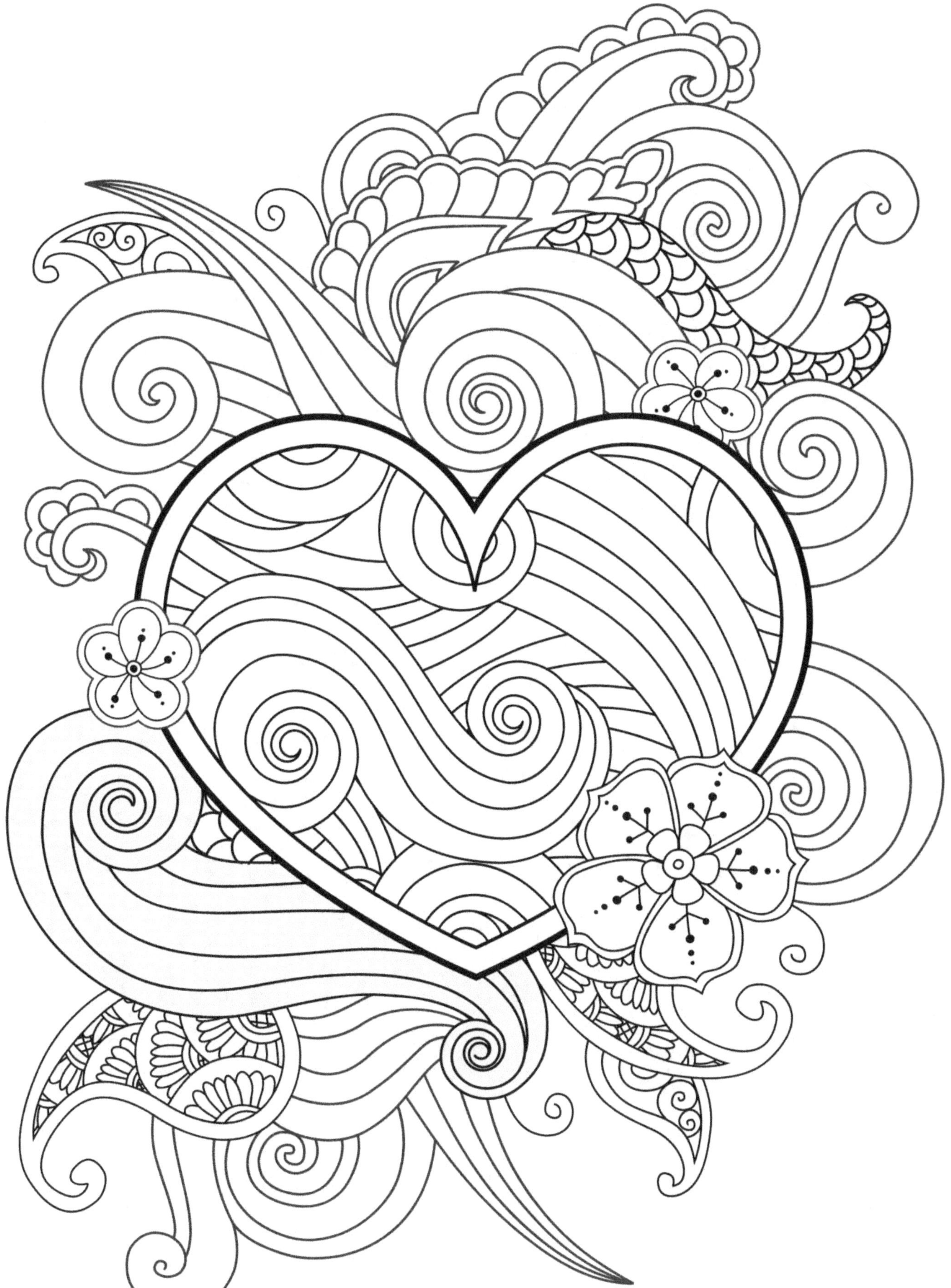

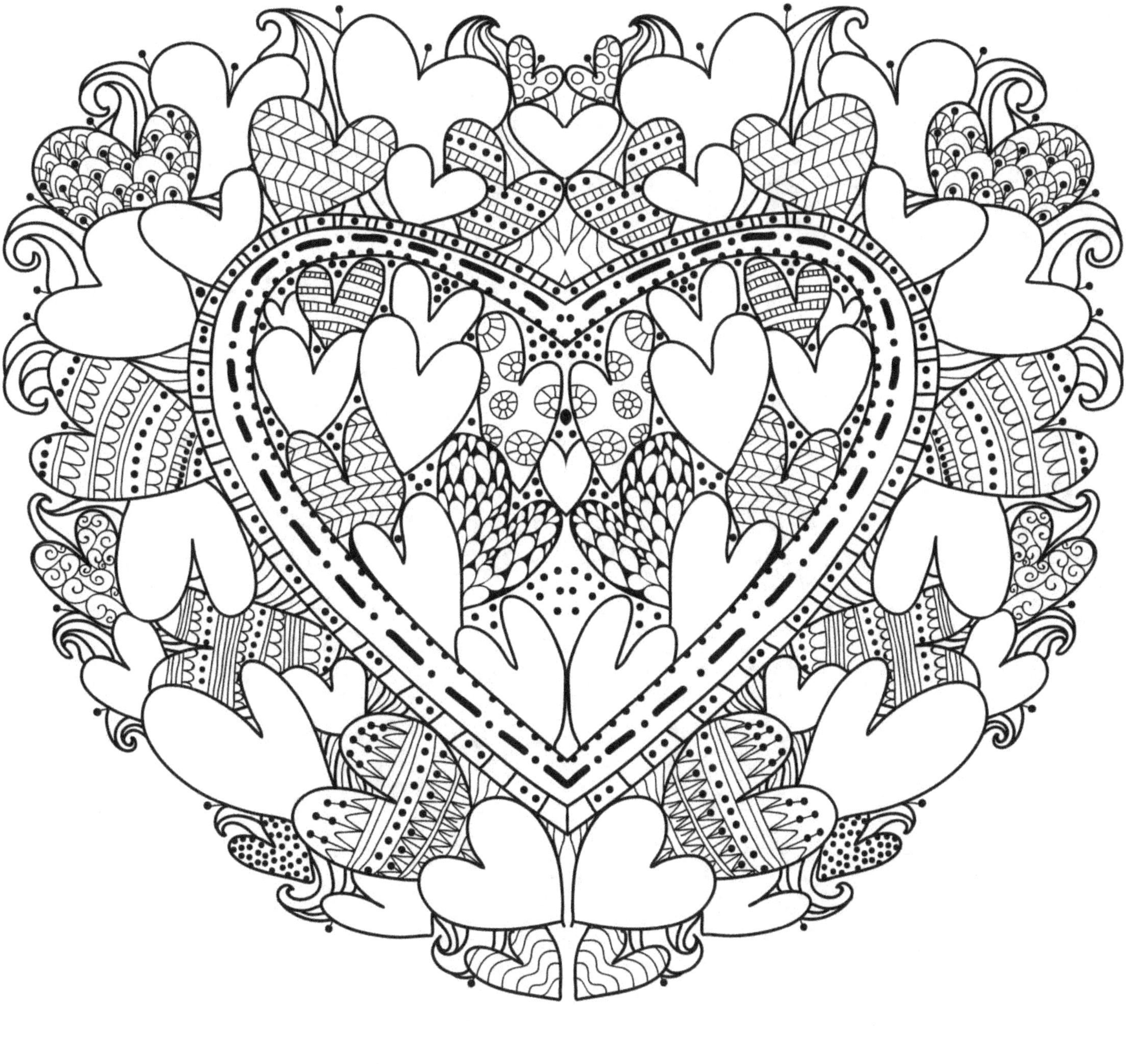

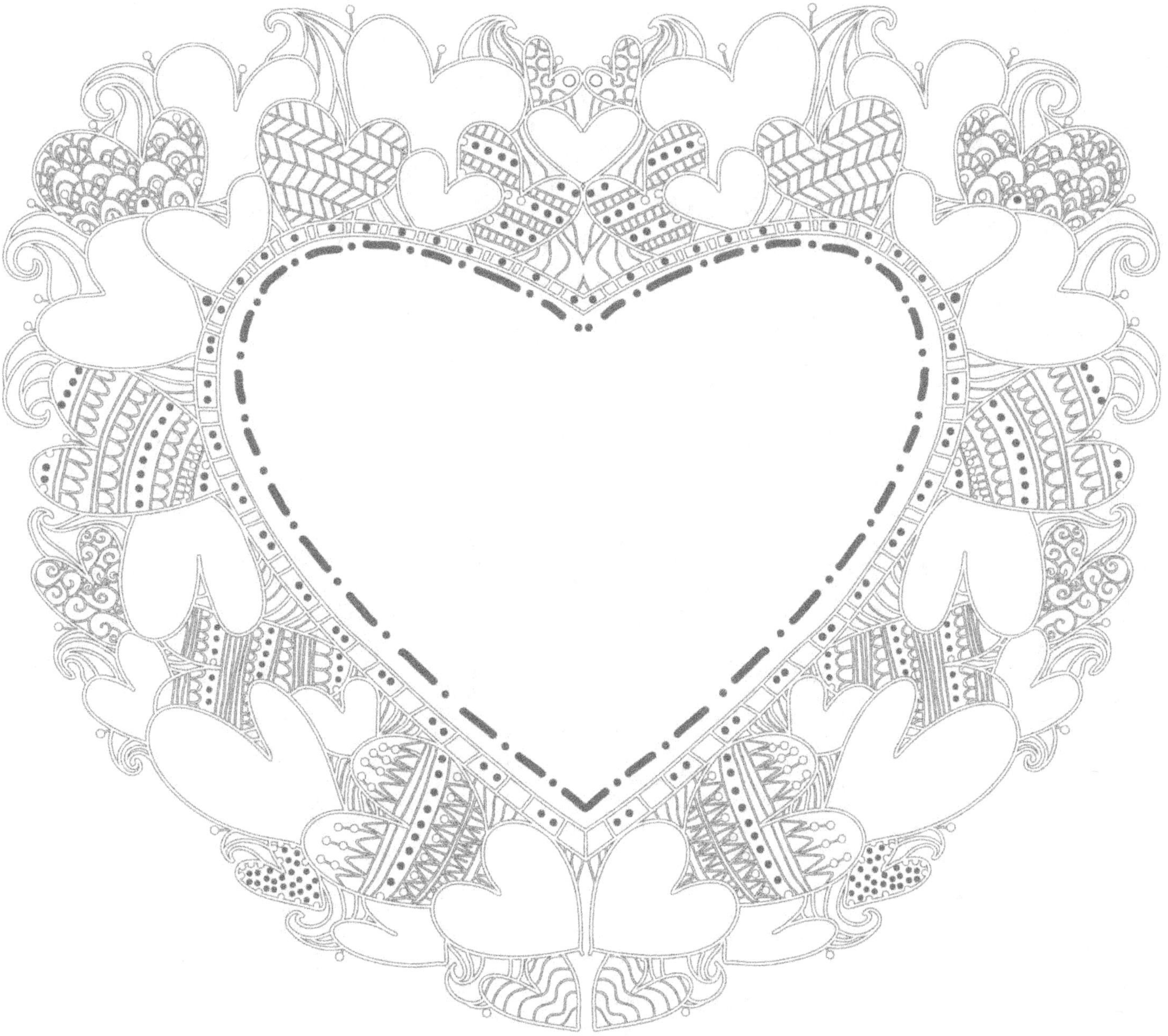

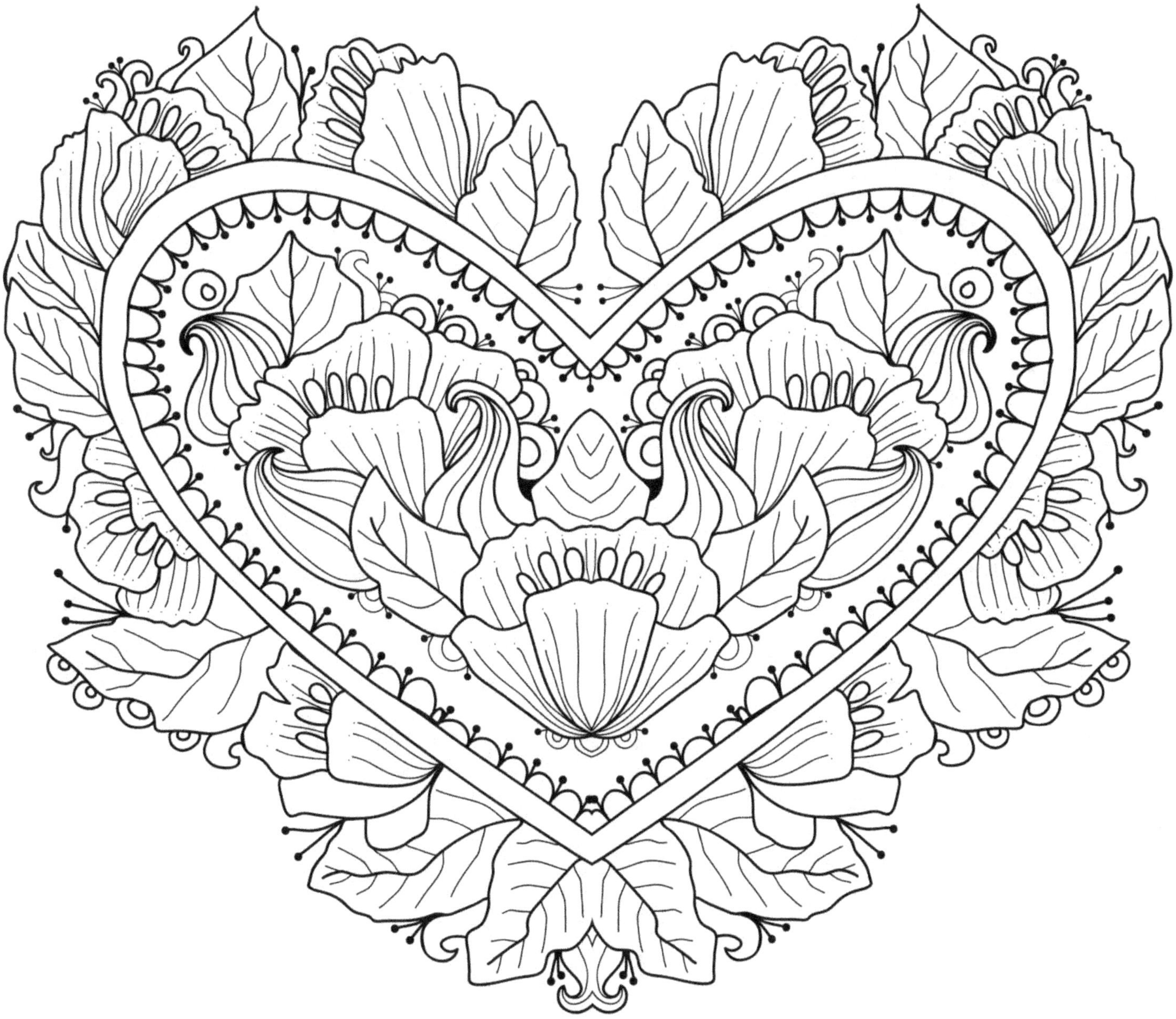

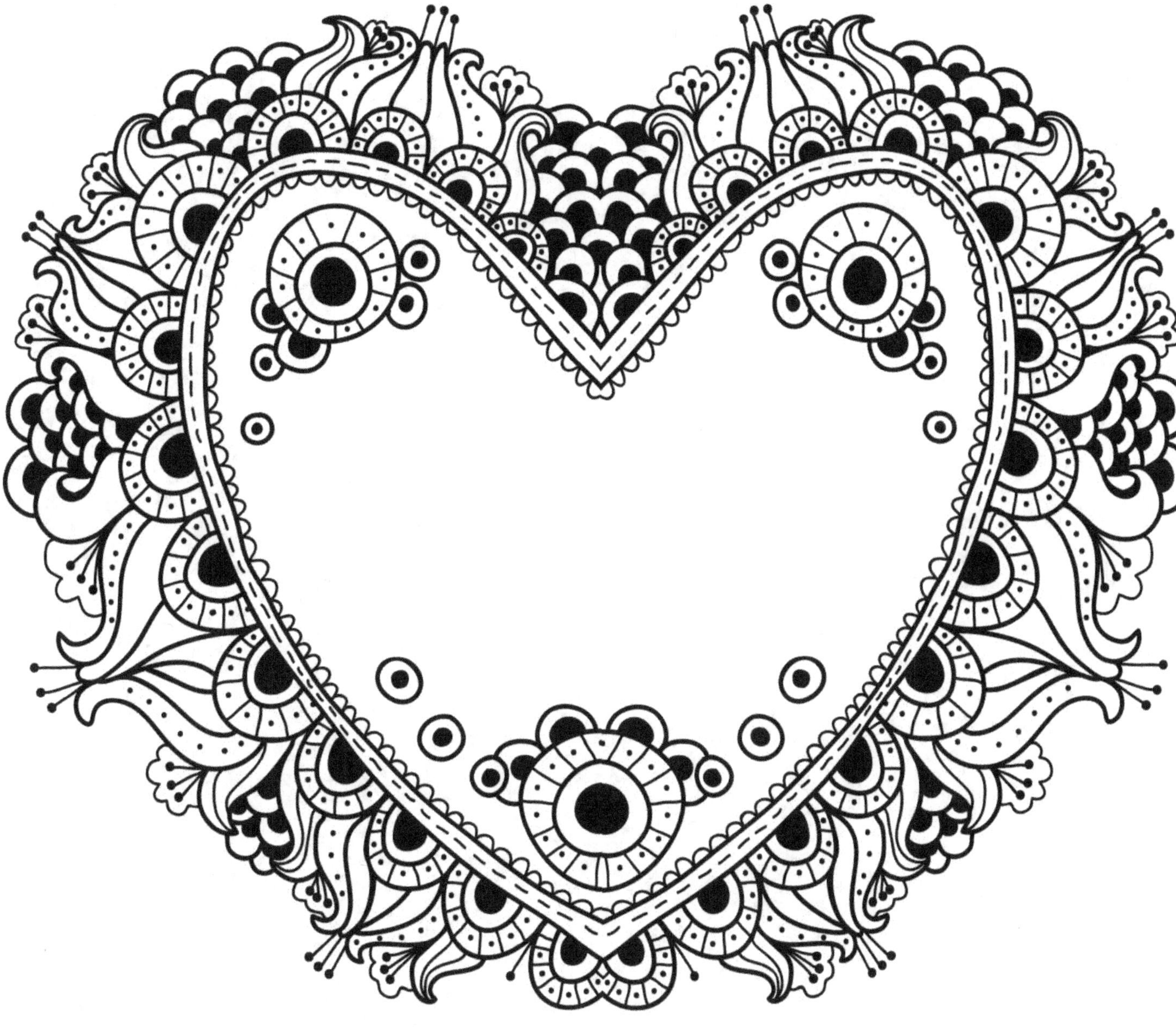

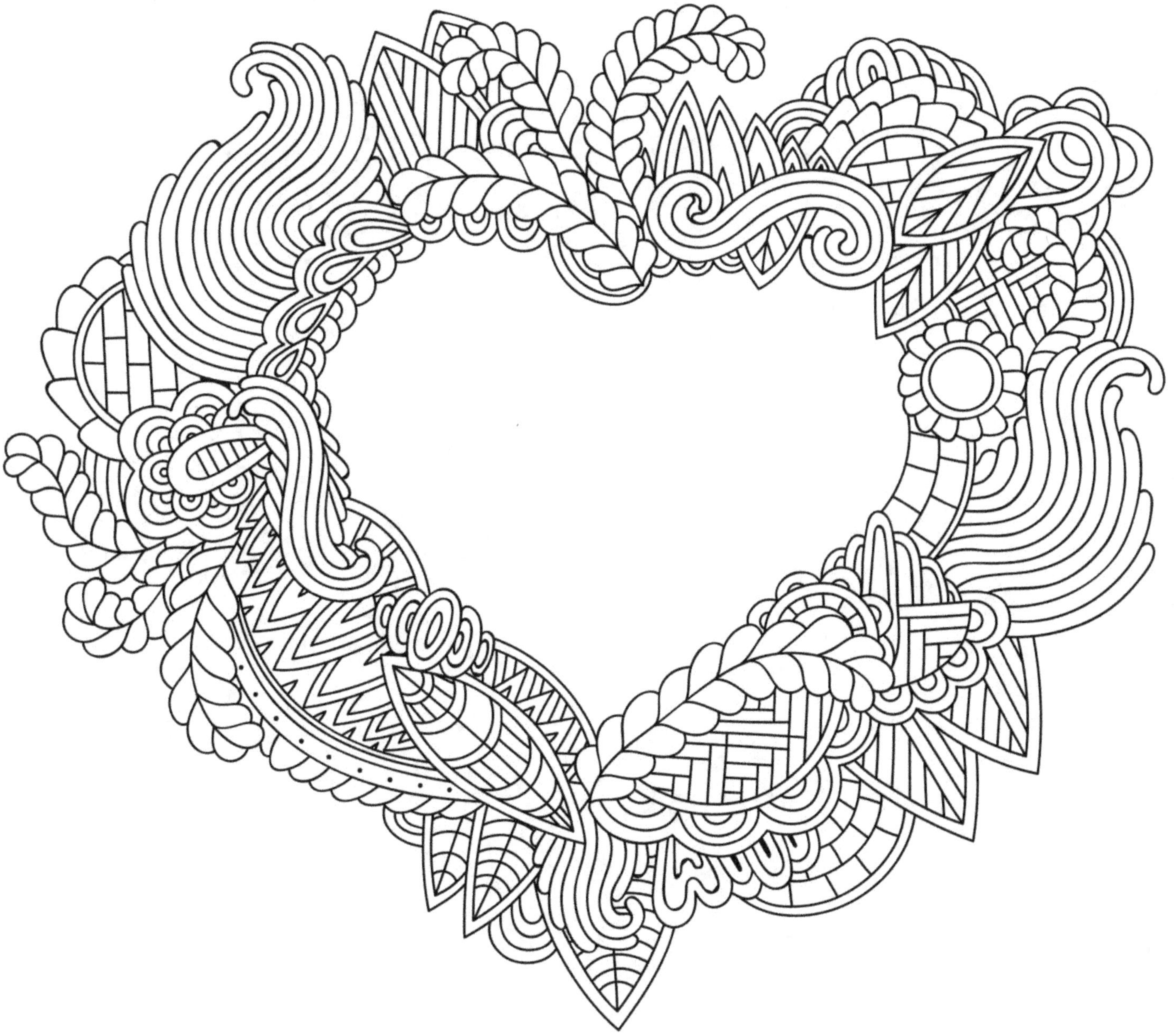

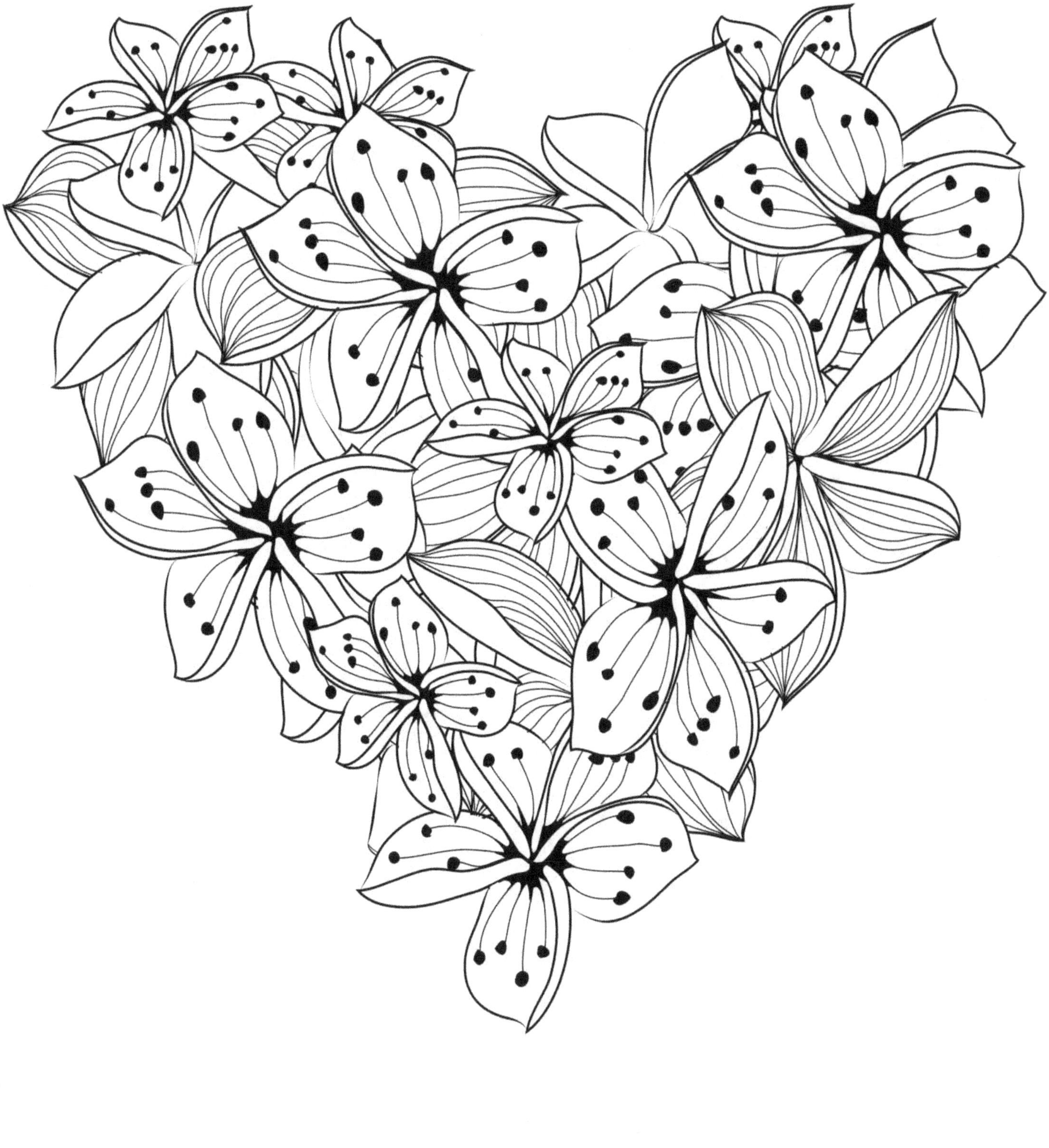

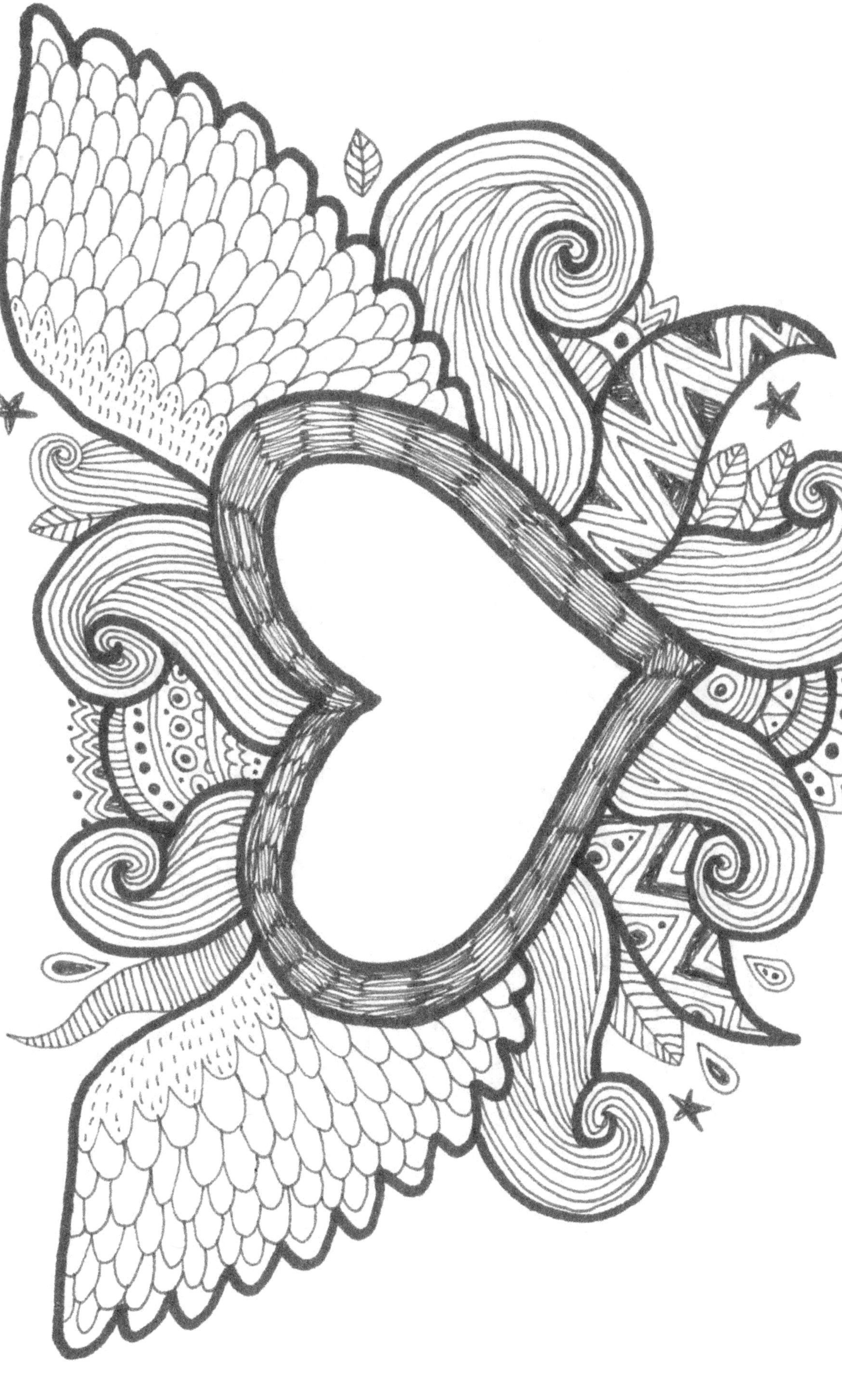

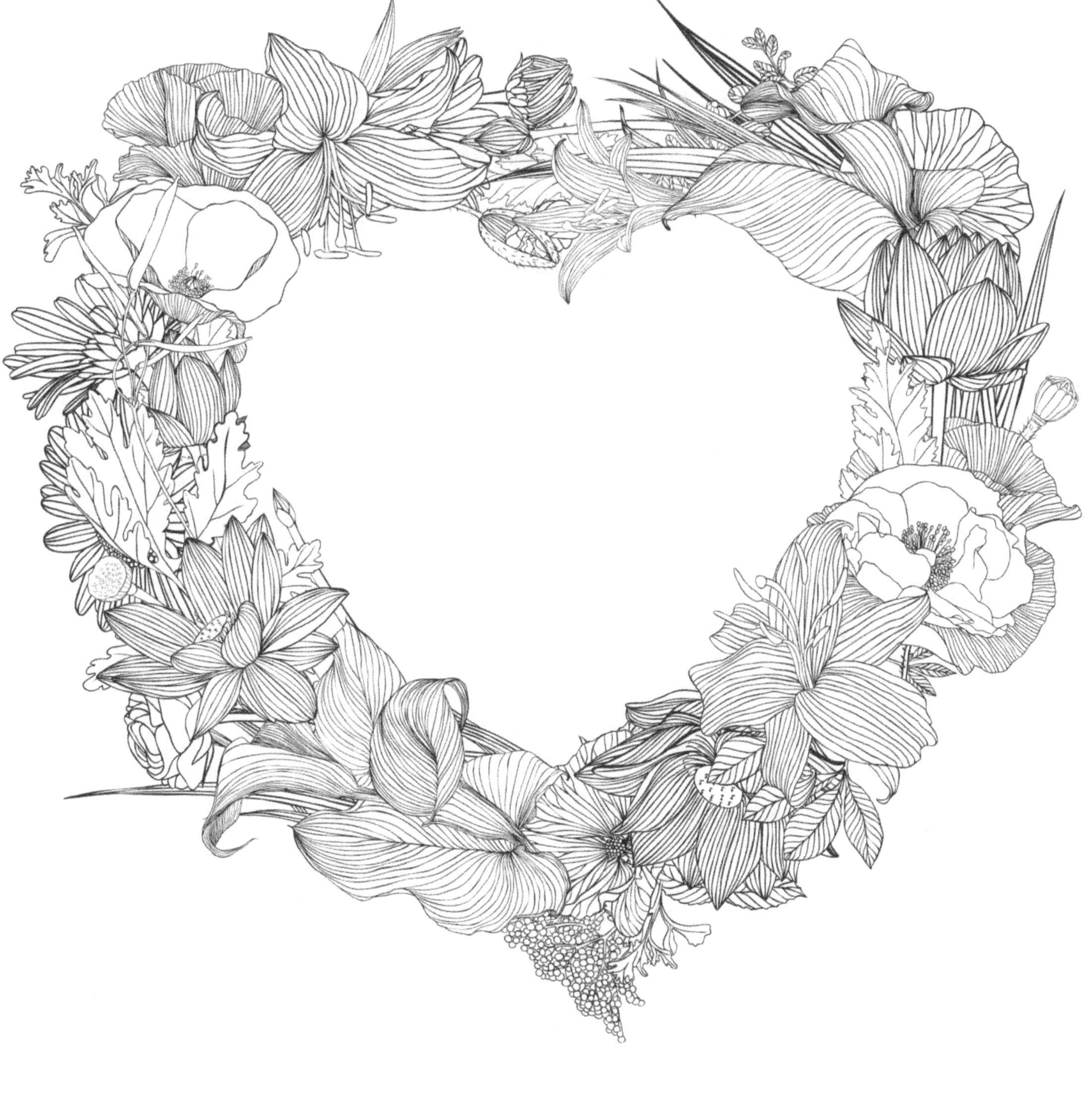

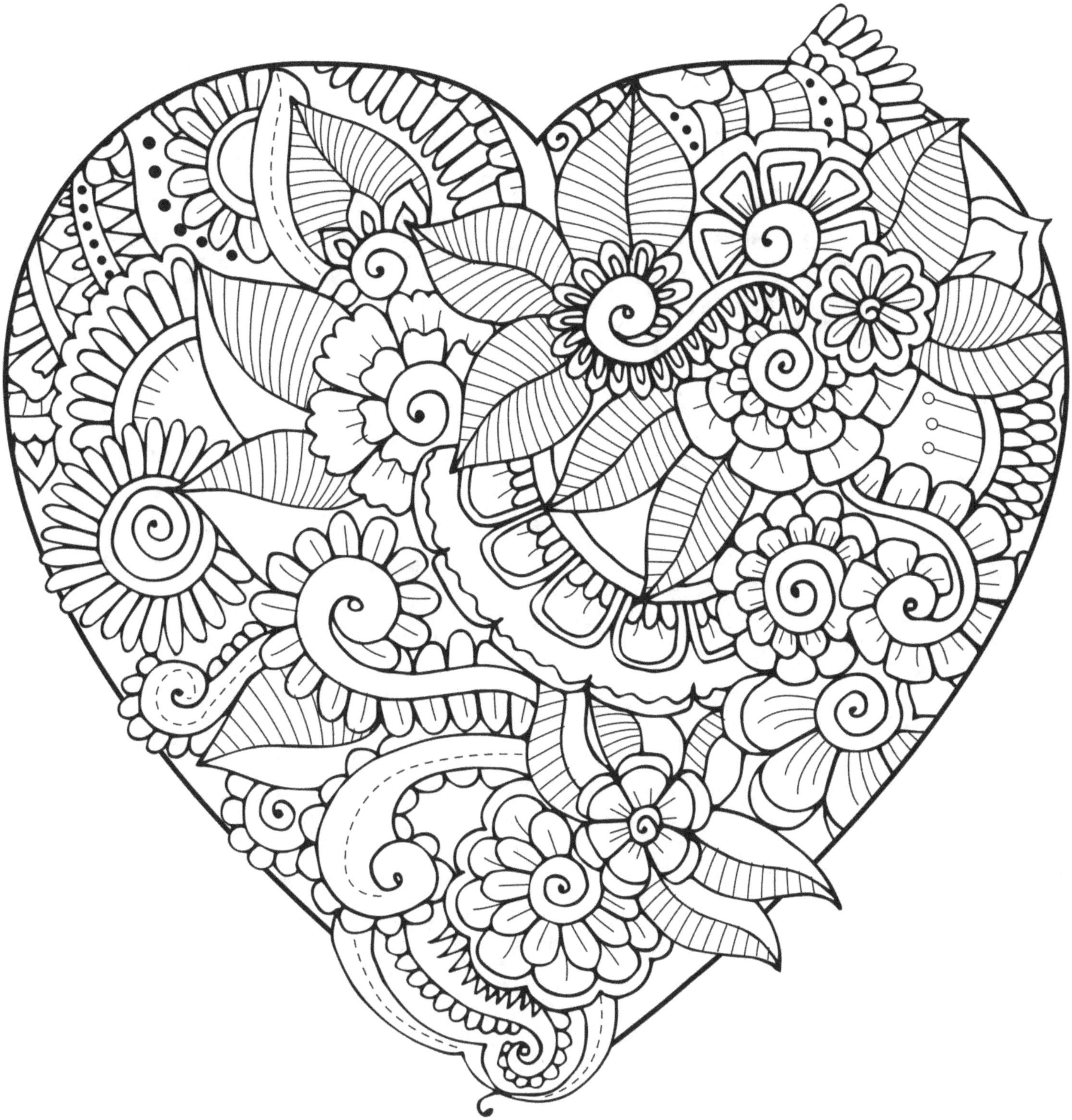

www.ingramcontent.com/pod-product-compliance
Lightning Source LLC
Chambersburg PA
CBHW081154280526
45787CB00008B/3330
* 9 7 8 1 5 4 8 0 2 3 0 7 2 *